SHORT WALKS
MADE EASY

NORTH PENNINES

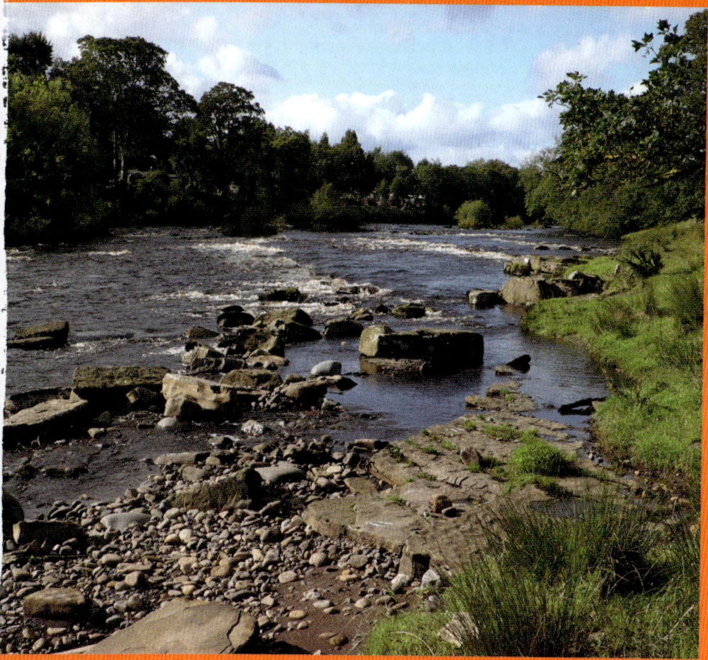

Ordnance Survey

Contents

	Getting outside in the North Pennines	6
	We smile more when we're outside	8
	Respecting the countryside	10
	Using this guide	11
Walk 1	Allen Banks	**14**
Walk 2	Geltsdale	**20**
Photos	Scenes from the walks	26
Walk 3	Blanchland	**28**
Walk 4	Alston	**34**
Photos	Wildlife interest	40
Walk 5	Long Meg and Her Daughters	**42**
Walk 6	River Wear at Stanhope	**48**
Walk 7	Dufton	**54**
Photos	Cafés and pubs	60
Walk 8	High Force and Low Force	**62**
Walk 9	Hury Reservoir	**68**
Walk 10	River Tees at Barnard Castle	**74**
	Credits	80

Map symbols	Front cover flap
Accessibility and what to take	Back cover flap
Walk locations	Inside front cover
Your next adventure?	Inside back cover

2 Short Walks Made Easy

Walk 1
ALLEN BANKS

Distance
2 miles / 3.2km

Time
1¼ hours

Start/Finish
Allen Banks (NT)

Parking NE47 7BP
National Trust car park

Cafés/pubs
Picnic benches

Wooded gorge: visit for bluebells in spring and tree colour in autumn

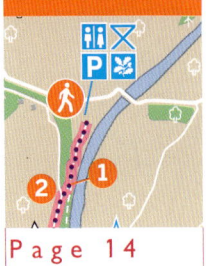

Page 14

Walk 2
GELTSDALE

Distance
2.6 miles / 4.2 km

Time
1½ hours

Start/Finish
RSPB Geltsdale

Parking CA8 2PW
RSPB Geltsdale car park

Cafés/pubs
Self-service at visitor centre

Rugged beauty: open moorland, meadows, a tarn; RSPB visitor centre

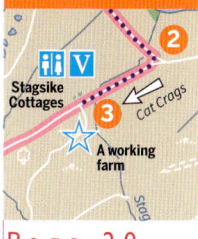

Page 20

Walk 3
BLANCHLAND

Distance
3.25 miles / 5.2 km

Time
2 hours CATCH A BUS

Start/Finish
Blanchland

Parking DH8 9TA
Blanchland car park

Cafés/pubs
White Monk Refectory/Tearoom; Lord Crewe Arms

Attractive village, pub and tearoom; engine house and abbey ruin

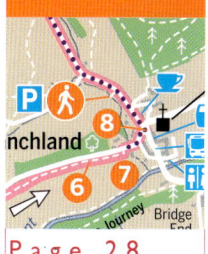

Page 28

Walk 4
ALSTON

Distance
2.1 miles / 3.4 km

Time
1¼ hours CATCH A BUS

Start/Finish
Alston

Parking CA9 3SN
Fairhill Recreation Ground car park

Cafés/pubs
Alston; café at South Tynedale Railway

Tourist steam railway; film/TV locations; an unlucky Market Cross

Page 34

Walk 5

LONG MEG AND HER DAUGHTERS

Distance
2.4 miles/3.8km

Time
1¼ hours

Start/Finish
Near Little Salkeld

Parking CA10 1NW
Long Meg and Her Daughters car park

Cafés/pubs
Nearest in Langwathby

One of Britain's largest stone circles; Norse tombstone; hedgerows

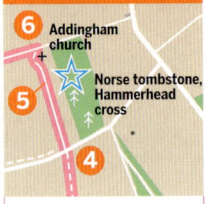

Page 42

Walk 6

RIVER WEAR AT STANHOPE

Distance
2.2 miles/3.5km

Time
1¼ hours *CATCH A BUS*

Start/Finish
Stanhope

Parking DL13 2FJ
Durham Dales Centre car park

Cafés/pubs
Durham Dales Centre; Stanhope

Attractive town and river stroll beside the Wear; fossil tree trunk

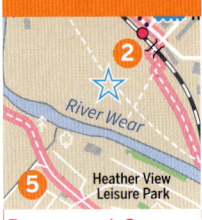

Page 48

Walk 7

DUFTON

Distance
2.1 miles/3.3km

Time
1¼ hours

Start/Finish
Dufton

Parking CA16 6DB
Dufton village car park

Cafés/pubs
Post Box Pantry café; The Stag Inn

Sample the Pennine Way; summit views; Dufton Ghyll Wood

Page 54

4 Short Walks Made Easy

Walk 8

HIGH FORCE AND LOW FORCE

Distance
3.9 miles/6.3km

Time
2¼ hours

Start/Finish
Bowlees

Parking DL12 0XE
Bowlees Visitor Centre car park

Cafés/pubs
Café at Bowlees Visitor Centre

River Tees, whitewater and spectacular falls; old suspension bridge

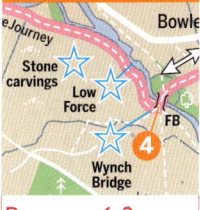

Page 62

Walk 9

HURY RESERVOIR

Distance
3 miles/4.8km

Time
1½ hours

Start/Finish
Near Hury in Baldersdale

Parking DL12 9UU
Car park at northern end of main reservoir dam

Cafés/pubs
Picnic tables

Reservoir circuit on the shore path; waterfowl; colourful meadows

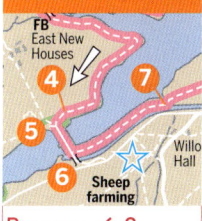

Page 68

Walk 10

RIVER TEES AT BARNARD CASTLE

Distance
4.4 miles/7.1km

Time
2½ hours   *CATCH A BUS*

Start/Finish
Barnard Castle

Parking DL12 8JJ
Galgate pay & display car park, beside Morrisons

Cafés/pubs
Barnard Castle

Lovely tree-lined riverside path; Egglestone Abbey; Butter Market

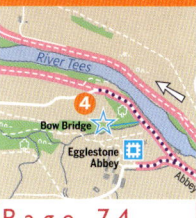

Page 74

GETTING OUTSIDE IN THE NORTH PENNINES

> **"** a beautiful landscape of rugged fells and upland commons incised by gentler dales, with copses and meadows

OS Champion
Mohammed Dhalech

Dufton Ghyll

A very warm welcome to the new Short Walks Made Easy guide to the North Pennines – what a fantastic selection of leisurely walks we have for you!

The North Pennines National Landscape was designated in 1988. Formerly an Area of Outstanding Natural Beauty, Britain's AONBs were re-termed National Landscapes in November 2023. Covering an area of almost 770 square miles, the North Pennines is the second largest National Landscape after the Cotswolds.

The open heather moor and peatland countryside has been carved into by fast-flowing rivers, like the Wear and the Tees and their tributaries, to create a beautiful landscape of rugged fells and upland commons incised by gentler dales, with copses and meadows. There's a rich mining and industrial heritage, a diverse African history at Allen Banks, and attractive market towns and villages. Since 2015, the North Pennines has been a UNESCO Geopark.

Walks in this guide lead you to wonderful natural spectacles, like High Force in Teesdale; to great views of the high Pennine summits from Dufton; and through peaceful, remote Geltsdale and its RSPB reserve. You can enjoy the charms of Blanchland, famed as one of England's prettiest villages; relish bluebells in spring and golden autumn colours in the wooded gorge of Allen Banks; and visit one of the largest Neolithic stone circles in Britain. See a fossilized tree trunk at Stanhope, complete a circuit of Hury Reservoir, and have fun on the steam railway at Alston.

Mohammed Dhalech,
OS Champion

WE SMILE MORE WHEN WE'RE OUTSIDE

Geltsdale

Whether it's a short walk during our lunch break or a full day's outdoor adventure, we know that a good dose of fresh air is just the tonic we all need.

At Ordnance Survey (OS), we're passionate about helping more people to get outside more often. It sits at the heart of everything we do, and through our products and services, we aim to help you lead an active outdoor lifestyle, so that you can live longer, stay younger and enjoy life more.

We firmly believe the outdoors is for everyone, and we want to help you find the very best Great Britain has to offer. We are blessed with an island that is beautiful and unique, with a rich and varied landscape. There are coastal paths to meander along, woodlands to explore, countryside to roam, and cities to uncover. Our trusted source of inspirational content is bursting with ideas for places to go, things to do and easy beginner's guides on how to get started.

It can be daunting when you're new to something, so we want to bring you the know-how from the people who live and breathe the outdoors. To help guide us, our team of awe-inspiring OS Champions share their favourite places to visit, hints and tips for outdoor adventures, as well as tried and tested accessible, family- and wheelchair-friendly routes. We hope that you will feel inspired to spend more time outside and reap the physical and mental health benefits that the outdoors has to offer. With our handy guides, paper and digital mapping, and exciting new apps, we can be with you every step of the way.

To find out more visit os.uk/getoutside

RESPECTING
THE COUNTRYSIDE

You can't beat getting outside in the British countryside, but it's vital that we leave no trace when we're enjoying the great outdoors.

Let's make sure that generations to come can enjoy the countryside just as we do.

 Leave no trace

 Keep dogs under control; bin and bag waste

 Do not light fires; only BBQ at official sites

 Leave gates as you find them

 Keep to footpaths and open access land

 Plan ahead for your trip

For more details please visit gov.uk/countryside-code

USING THIS GUIDE

Easy-to-follow North Pennine walks for all

Before setting off

Check the walk information panel to plan your outing

- Consider using **Public transport** where flagged. If driving, note the satnav postcode for the car park under **Parking**
- The suggested **Time** is based on a gentle pace
- Note the availability of **Cafés**, tearooms and pubs, and **Toilets**

Terrain and hilliness

- **Terrain** indicates the nature of the route surface
- Any rises and falls are noted under **Hilliness**

Walking with your dog?

- This panel states where **Dogs** *must* be on a lead and how many stiles there are – in case you need to lift your dog
- Keep dogs on leads where there are livestock and between April and August in forest and on moorland where there are ground-nesting birds

A perfectly pocket-sized walking guide

- Handily sized for ease of use on each walk
- When not being read, it fits nicely into a pocket…
- …so between points, put this book in the pocket of your coat, trousers or day sack and enjoy your stroll in glorious countryside – we've made it pocket-sized for a reason!

Flexibility of route presentation to suit all readers

- **Not comfortable map reading?** Then use the simple-to-follow route profile and accompanying route description and pictures
- **Happy to map read?** New-look walk mapping makes it easier for you to focus on the route and the points of interest along the way
- **Read the insightful Did you know?, Local legend, Stories behind the walk** and **Nature notes** to help you make the most of your day out and to enjoy all that each walk has to offer

OS information about the walk

- Many of the features and symbols shown are taken from Ordnance Survey's celebrated **Explorer** mapping, designed to help people across Great Britain enjoy leisure time spent outside

- National Grid reference for the start point
- Explorer sheet map covering the route

OS information
🚶 NY 798640
Explorer OL43

The easy-to-use walk map

- **Large-scale** mapping for ultra-clear route finding

- **Numbered points** at key turns along the route that tie in with the route instructions and respective points marked on the profile

- **Pictorial symbols** for intuitive map reading, see Map Symbols on the front cover flap

The simple-to-follow walk profile

- Progress easily along the route using the illustrative profile, it has **numbered points** for key turning points and **graduated distance markers**

- Easy-read **route directions** with turn-by-turn detail

- Reassuring **route photographs** for each numbered point

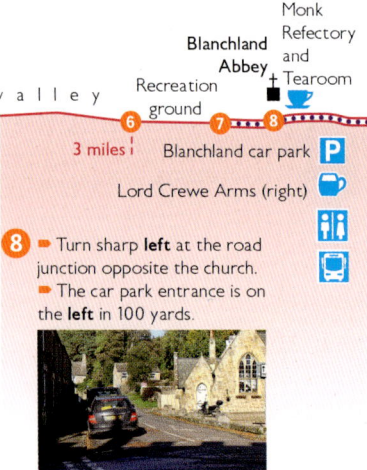

12 Short Walks Made Easy

Using QR codes

- Scan each QR code to see the route in Ordnance Survey's OS Maps App
NB You may need to download a scanning app if you have an older phone

- OS Maps will open the route automatically if you have it installed. If not, the route will open in the web version of OS Maps

- Please click **Start Route** button to begin navigating or **Download Route** to store the route for offline use

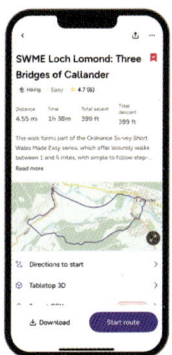

North Pennines

WALK 1

ALLEN BANKS

Having thundered down from the Pennine moors, the two branches of the River Allen unite to carve a deep cleft through the Northumberland countryside. The banks of the gorge are cloaked with oak, beech, yew and sycamore, making it the county's largest ancient woodland. During the 19th century, landowner Susan Davidson created a network of paths here, trails that are today maintained by the National Trust, enabling visitors to explore this impressive landscape and enjoy its diverse wildlife (nationaltrust.org.uk).

OS information
NY 798640 Explorer OL43
Distance 2 miles/3.2km
Time 1¼ hours
Start/Finish Allen Banks (NT)
Parking NE47 7BP National Trust car park, signposted south off the A69, 1¼ miles east of Bardon Mill
Public toilets In the car park
Cafés/pubs Picnic benches. Nearest café is the Village Store and Tearoom, Bardon Mill
Terrain Woodland paths, mostly well maintained; steps at ❺
Hilliness Undulating with some short, steep sections
Footwear Winter/Spring/Autumn 🥾 Summer 👟

Public transport

Nearest bus stop is on the A69/Ridley Hall road junction, ⅔ mile from 🚶 for bus service 685, Hexham to Brampton: stagecoachbus.com

Accessibility

Robust, powered wheelchairs and all-terrain pushchairs 🚶 to ❺ and ❻ to end (one steep incline after ❶)

Dogs

Welcome on leads. No stiles

Did you know? The John Martin Heritage Trail passes through Allen Banks. Born in Bardon Mill in 1789, Martin was best known for his paintings and engravings of religious subjects often set in dramatic landscapes. He is said to have been heavily influenced by the geology and terrain of his native Northumberland. His work is on display in the Laing Art Gallery in Newcastle and London's Tate Britain.

Local legend A few miles upstream of the National Trust car park are the ruined remains of Staward Peel, a medieval fortified house. No longer permanently inhabited in the early 18th century, it became a refuge for an itinerant livestock thief known as Dickie of Kingswood. Dickie is said to have travelled far to conduct his 'business', even stealing from Newcastle and then driving cattle across country to Cumberland to sell them.

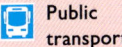

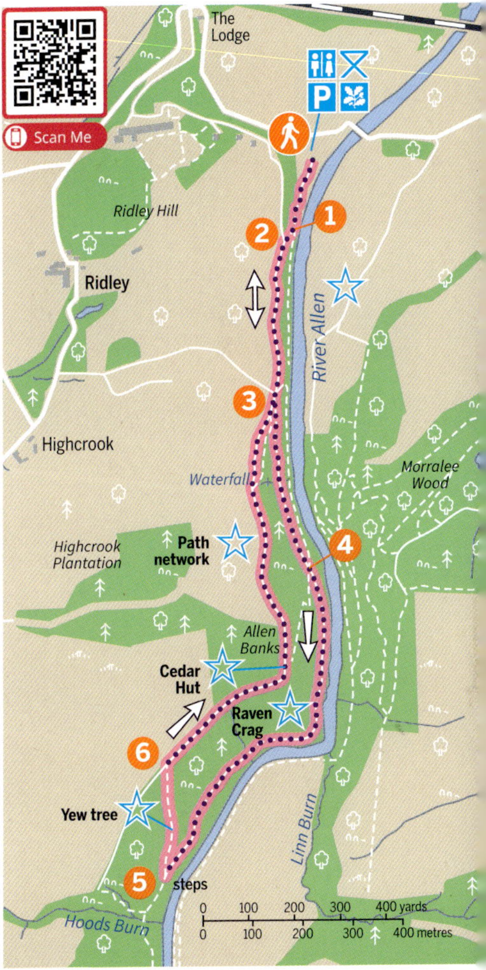

Walk 1 Allen Banks

STORIES BEHIND THE WALK

☆ **Path network** In the 1830s, John Davidson of Otterburn bought the estate that covers Allen Banks for his wife Susan. Over the next 35 years, she set about taming the landscape – creating flower beds in the nearby formal gardens, planting trees in the gorge, building bridges, revealing viewpoints and creating a network of paths through the woods. Many of those paths still exist and continue to be maintained by the National Trust, which has owned the woodland since 1942.

☆ **River Allen** In its upper reaches, the River Allen divides into two arms. The River East Allen rises on the moorland border of Northumberland and County Durham and passes through Allenheads and Allendale Town, once an important centre for lead mining and smelting. The River West Allen flows through a more sparsely inhabited valley. The two meet just south of Allen Banks and then enter the River South Tyne near Bardon Mill.

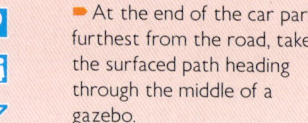

National Trust car park

- At the end of the car park furthest from the road, take the surfaced path heading through the middle of a gazebo.
- Follow this path for almost 150 yards to a fork, soon after entering trees.

1 ▪ Branch **right**, heading steeply uphill for a few paces – marked with orange and brown waymarkers – until the path splits again.

16 Short Walks Made Easy

⭐ Raven Crag

Located on a bend in the River Allen, the cliffs of Raven Crag tower over the riverside path. They are made up of beds of sandstone that formed in the Carboniferous period between 360 and 300 million years ago. At that time, this area was near the Equator and the sand formed part of a river delta that was intermittently covered by shallow tropical seas. Eventually, the sand hardened to form sandstone.

⭐ Cedar Hut

The Cedar Hut is located on high ground above Raven Crag on a bend in the River Allen. It is a reconstruction of Susan Davidson's 19th-century summerhouse, built here to take advantage of the foliage-framed views down the densely wooded slopes and higher up into the valley. Wooden seats at the back of the hut and a roof allow today's visitors to enjoy the location whatever the weather.

Raven Crag ⭐

4

River Allen

2 ▶ Take either option, although the right-hand route avoids steps.
▶ The two paths quickly reunite to skirt the top of a wooded embankment. Follow this to a fork in about 300 yards.

3 ▶ Bear **left** at the fork, staying on the lower path for 350 yards to another fork. (The higher path forms part of your return route.)

Walk 1 Allen Banks

NATURE NOTES

The most striking thing about Allen Banks is its dense woodland. Beech and oak are common species here, but there are also sycamore trees, Scots pine, yew, holly, lime and sweet chestnut, all contributing to the kaleidoscope of colours that becomes particularly vivid in the autumn. Watch for a particularly fine yew tree to the right of the path on the climb to ❻.

Autumn is also a good time for spotting the fungi that thrive in damp, dark corners of the woods. Species include giant puffball, sulphur tufts and oyster mushrooms.

In spring, parts of the woodland floor are carpeted with wildflowers such as bluebells, primroses, wood anemone and wild garlic, also known as ramsons.

When walking beside the river, watch for dippers bobbing up and down on the rocks, as well as grey wagtail, goosander and heron.

Yew near ❻

❹ ▸ Keep **left** again, soon dropping closer to the River Allen.
▸ Pass below Raven Crag at a bend in river.
▸ Carry on above the river for about ¼ mile then go down three steps.

❺ ▸ A few strides beyond the last of the three steps turn **right**, climbing a flight of steps and heading up a steep slope – still following the orange waymarked trail. Reach a T-junction at the top.

18 Short Walks Made Easy

Above: grey wagtail
Below: sulphur tuft

Top: beech leaves
Above: wild garlic
Below: primrose

½ miles

2 miles

6 ▸ Turn **right** at the junction, reaching the Cedar Hut summerhouse in 300 yards.
▸ About ⅓ mile beyond the summerhouse, the path drops back to **3**. Bear left to retrace your steps to the car park.

National Trust car park

Old beech tree

Walk 1 Allen Banks

WALK 2

GELTSDALE

Sitting at the foot of Cold Fell, the Pennines' northernmost summit, the RSPB's Geltsdale nature reserve has a rugged, bleak beauty about it. Habitats on this remote reserve include heather moorland, blanket bog, grassland, wetland, meadows and woods – home to a range of species, including rare birds such as hen harrier and black grouse. Keeping to low ground, this walk samples a tiny segment of what's on offer, passing meadows, an upland tarn and new woodland, and calling in at the visitor centre part-way round (rspb.org.uk).

OS information

NY 588584
Explorer OL43

Distance
2.6 miles/4.2km

Time
1½ hours

Start/Finish
RSPB Geltsdale

Parking CA8 2PW
RSPB Geltsdale car park (honesty box) at Clesketts, 1 mile south-east of A689 at Hallbankgate

Public toilets
At the visitor centre

Cafés/pubs
Self-service refreshment facilities at visitor centre; Hallbankgate Hub Café and Belted Will Inn, both in Hallbankgate

Terrain
Gravel tracks and grassy path

Hilliness
Gently undulating

Footwear
Winter/Spring/Autumn
Summer

Public transport
Nearest bus stop in Hallbankgate for service 680, Carlisle to Brampton (one bus in each direction, Mon-Fri): telfordscoaches.com

Accessibility

Robust powered wheelchairs from 🚶 to ③; suitable for all-terrain pushchairs but bumpier ground between ③ and ④

Dogs

Welcome but keep on leads. No stiles

Did you know? Stephenson's Rocket, one of the earliest steam locomotives, ended its working life on a mineral railway near Geltsdale. James Thompson of Kirkhouse bought it from the Liverpool and Manchester Railway in 1836 for £300. It operated in the area for the next four years and was then donated to London's Patent Office Museum in 1862. It is now on display in the National Railway Museum in York.

Local legend The level crossing at Miltonrigg Woods, near Hallbankgate, was the scene of a fatal accident in 1926. Nine people, including two young children, were killed when a passenger train crashed into a charabanc that had been erroneously allowed to cross the tracks. People have since reported hearing the ghostly cries of children coming from the crash site.

Walk 2 Geltsdale

STORIES BEHIND THE WALK

☆ **A working farm** The RSPB works with its tenant farmer on the reserve to encourage wildlife. Sensitive agricultural techniques include the introduction of blue-grey cattle and a reduction in the number of sheep on the moorland. The latter, combined with the blocking of artificial drains and the cessation of heather-burning, is helping the charity to restore blanket bogs, which play an important role in the fight against global warming.

V Stagsike Cottages
The Stagsike Cottages were converted into an RSPB office and visitor information point in 2007. The building is usually open from 9am to 5pm and, as well as information about the reserve and lists of recently spotted species, it houses self-service refreshment facilities and hosts exhibitions by local artists and photographers. There is also disabled parking here, toilets and picnic benches.

☆ Old crab apple tree

½ mile

RSPB Geltsdale car park

Gate/cattle gr

Small copper

- Start as if to walk back down the car park's access lane, but then go through a large gate on the **right**.
- A broad, stony track climbs gradually for ⅓ mile and then descends to a gate.

⭐ New woodland

Since about 2005, the RSPB has been planting open, scrubby woodland at the northern base of Cold Fell – the area between ③ and ④. Native trees such as rowan, hawthorn, hazel, juniper and downy birch are among the species that have been introduced here. These encourage a greater diversity of wildlife, including black grouse which seek woodland for breeding and winter feeding.

⭐ Howgill

The cottages at Howgill used to house miners and their families. Coal was mined in Geltsdale and surrounding areas from the 1820s onwards, much of it worked by the Thompson family of Kirkhouse under a lease from Lord Carlisle. The drift mine at Howgill was closed in 1880, although sections of it were then reopened in the 20th century.

Stagsike Cottages

1 mile

⭐ A working farm

① ➤ Go through the gate beside a cattle grid and continue along the track.
➤ As the track swings **right** towards Stagsike Cottages visitor centre, ignore the gated track on the left.

② ➤ Swing **right** again at the top of a short rise, as a fainter path joins from the left.
➤ The level track makes its way towards the visitor centre, passing through a gate just before reaching it.

NATURE NOTES

Geltsdale is home to a very wide range of birds, including various waders: watch for snipe, redshank, lapwing and curlew. Easily identified by its long, curved beak, the curlew is the largest wading bird found in Britain. Tindale Tarn is home to Canada geese, greylag geese, tufted duck, coot and mute swans. The latter is the only species of native swan that stays in Britain all year round. The bird feeders at the visitor centre are a good place for spotting tits and finches, including goldfinches.

The grassland and meadows are rich with grasses, thistles, knapweed, meadow buttercups and yarrow, all helping other species to thrive, including small mammals, farmland birds and butterflies such as the common blue, small skipper, large skipper, small copper, dark green fritillary, red admiral and peacock.

As the track begins heading downhill towards ❶, watch for a solitary old crab apple tree to the left.

Old crab apple tree

Howgill

New woodland (left)

1½ miles

❸ ▶ Beyond the visitor centre, keep **straight ahead** on a broad, grassy path.
▶ This later crosses two small bridges and then climbs steadily towards cottages at Howgill.
▶ Approaching a large gate near Howgill, ignore the signposted trail to the left; instead, go through the gate.

24 Short Walks Made Easy

Curlew

Left: goldfinch **Middle:** mute swan **Right:** yarrow

2 miles

2½ miles | RSPB Geltsdale car park 🅿

④ ➤ Immediately turn **right**, through a second gate.
➤ The track leads back to the car park in ¾ mile.

Small skipper

Walk 2 Geltsdale 25

This page (clockwise): moorland track and Pennypie House, near Blanchland; River Tees near Low Force; Market Place, Alston; ancient woodland at Allen Banks
Opposite (clockwise): fountain on Dufton village green; Hammerhead cross, Addingham church; Hury Reservoir

WALK 3

BLANCHLAND

The historic village of Blanchland lies in a riverside hollow on Northumberland's border with County Durham. White-robed monks first built an abbey here in 1165 and today it is conserved as part of a charity established by the Bishop of Durham in the 18th century. It is a great place for exploring on foot, home to tree-lined valley paths and moorland tracks. This walk enjoys the best of both, combining a short section of higher ground with a stroll near the River Derwent (blanchland.org).

OS information

NY 964504
Explorer OL43

Distance
3.25 miles/5.2km

Time
2 hours

Start/Finish
Blanchland

Parking DH8 9TA
Blanchland car park (honesty box), Shildon Road

Public toilets
By the Derwent road bridge (B6303), just south of 8

Cafés/pubs
White Monk Refectory and Tearoom, and Lord Crewe Arms, both in Blanchland

Terrain
Asphalt lanes; moorland track; good valley path

Hilliness
Steady climb to 3; steeper descent 4 to 5

Did you know? Blanchland has been used as a setting for several films and TV series. Films include *Jude*, based on Thomas Hardy's novel, *Jude the Obscure*, and an adaptation of Catherine Cookson's *The Gambling Man*. More recently, the gatehouse and square featured in the TV series *Wolfblood* and in episodes of *Vera*, the crime drama series set in the north-east of England.

Local legend During a 16th-century raid by Scots, Blanchland's monks resorted to desperate prayers. A heavy fog descended, making it impossible for the Scots to find the abbey. Prematurely celebrating their escape, the monks rang the bells, but the departing raiders heard the noise, turned around and followed the sound to the abbey. They killed some of the monks and tried to burn down the building.

Footwear
Year round

Public transport
Bus service 773, Consett to Townfield (two buses in each direction, Mon-Fri): weardale-travel.co.uk

Accessibility
Robust, all-terrain wheelchairs and pushchairs from to 2 and from 7 to end

Dogs
Welcome but keep on leads. No stiles

Walk 3 Blanchland

STORIES BEHIND THE WALK

☆ **Shildon Engine House** Constructed in Birmingham in 1808, Shildon Engine House was designed to help prevent local lead mines from flooding. The building was transported north via canals, the sea and then with teams of ponies; but was used for less than 10 years because the mine was deemed unprofitable. It was converted to miners' accommodation in 1861, was in ruins by the start of the 20th century and was then partially restored in 2010 (historicengland.org.uk).

☆ **Pennypie House** This Grade II-listed farmhouse occupies a lonely spot on the moorland above Blanchland. It dates mostly from the 18th century, although alterations were made during the 19th century. It was once an inn and is said to have got its name from the pies the innkeeper sold to passing drovers and mineworkers for just a single penny.

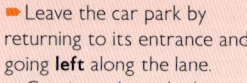

Shildon Burn valley — ½ mile — ☆ Shildon Engine House — ① Shildon

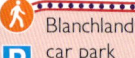

Blanchland car park

► Leave the car park by returning to its entrance and going **left** along the lane.
► Continue along the lane for ½ mile to a small gate on the left.

① ► Go through the small gate for access to the Shildon Engine House viewpoint.
► Having visited, return to the surfaced lane and continue **uphill** for another ¾ mile to a track junction near Pennypie House.

30 Short Walks Made Easy

☆ **Drystone walls** As in much of the rest of the North Pennines, drystone walls are a common feature of the countryside around Blanchland. Some walls date from medieval times, although long, straight walls typical of the higher ground are more closely associated with the Enclosure Acts of the 18th and 19th centuries. Note how the walls have been built without any mortar; stability is achieved through traditional construction methods.

☩ Blanchland Abbey

The parish church of St Mary's is all that remains of the abbey church established by Premonstratensian monks in 1165, although many parts of the building date from later periods. Visitors to the village can also see the abbey gateway and the prior's house, which is now the Lord Crewe Arms pub. Many of Blanchland's other beautiful buildings were made using the stones of the original abbey.

Pennypie House ☆

1 mile ··· ② ··· 1½ miles

Ford, Shildon Burn

Burn valley — Moorland

②
- As the track bends right at Pennypie House, turn **left**.
- In a few strides, turn **left** again at a track T-junction to cross Shildon Burn.
- Continue ascending over the moor for ⅔ mile until you reach a fork in the track, near a fingerpost.

③
- Keep **left** at the fork to reach a surfaced lane in 75 yards, passing the fingerpost and a compound surrounded by trees (right).

Walk 3 Blanchland

NATURE NOTES

This walk passes through two strikingly different habitats. First, there is the wooded valley of Shildon Burn, followed by open heather moorland before returning to a wooded path, this time in the Derwent valley.

Shildon Burn's slopes are cloaked in a variety of trees, including horse chestnut, hazel, rowan, birch, beech, oak, sycamore and various conifers, including Scots pine. Where the canopy is less dense, bracken thrives. There's a good chance of spotting roe deer among the trees if you're here early or late in the day. The woodland strip encountered towards the end of the walk also features sweet chestnut.

The moorland, on the other hand, is dominated by heather – with not much else, and it is managed for grouse shooting. Red grouse tend to conceal themselves among the heather, and if they happen to be foraging near the track try not to be alarmed if they suddenly burst into flight or if you hear them cackling loudly nearby. The moorland edges are fringed by bracken and gorse.

Red grouse

Drystone walls 3 4
Moorland   2 miles

4 ▶ Go **left** down the lane.
▶ Leaving the open moorland, the lane heads downhill, steeply at times, to a T-junction in the valley bottom.

5 ▶ At the junction, cross diagonally **left** to join a permissive path (which starts to the left of a field gate).
▶ Keep **ahead** for ⅓ mile to a fork.

6 ▶ Bear **right** at the fork.
▶ Walk along the left-hand edge of a recreation ground to a kissing-gate on the far side.

Top left: bracken
Above: sweet chestnut
Bottom left: roe deer
Below: rowan berries

Derwent valley

2½ miles   3 miles

White Monk Refectory and Tearoom
Blanchland Abbey
Recreation ground
Blanchland car park
Lord Crewe Arms (right)

7 ➤ Go through the kissing-gate to enter a parking area.
➤ Immediately bear **left** to leave it and turn **right** along a road to a junction in the centre of Blanchland, opposite the abbey church.

8 ➤ Turn sharp **left** at the road junction opposite the church.
➤ The car park entrance is on the **left** in 100 yards.

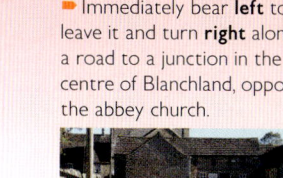

Walk 3 Blanchland   33

WALK 4

ALSTON

Alston is one of the two highest market towns in England, with much of it located at about 1,050 feet above sea level. Wandering its quiet alleyways and cobbled lanes, while gazing up at its many 17th-century buildings, is like stepping back in time but without the bustle associated with the lead mining that prompted its growth. This walk explores the town and part of the surrounding countryside, including a short section of the Pennine Way beside the River South Tyne.

OS information
NY 721462 Explorer OL31
Distance 2.1 miles / 3.4 km
Time 1¼ hours
Start/Finish Alston
Parking CA9 3SN Fairhill Recreation Ground car park, Nenthead Road
Public toilets Behind the town hall, Front Street
Cafés/pubs Alston; Hickins' at the Crossing Café, South Tynedale Railway
Terrain Town pavements, cobbles and alleys; field path; woodland trails
Hilliness Brief steep descent after ③; steady climb back through the town from ⑥
Footwear Year round
Public transport Bus service 681, between Haltwhistle and Alston: gonortheast.co.uk

34 Short Walks Made Easy

Did you know? Much of the current market cross in the middle of Alston was constructed in the 1980s. The previous one had been destroyed by a runaway lorry. The one that was demolished had been a replacement for a 19th-century market cross that had also been destroyed by a lorry! That one replaced the original built in 1765 by William Stephenson, the Lord Mayor of London who was born in Alston.

Local legend Front Street's Angel Inn, which was built in 1611, is said to be haunted by a former landlady who died more than 100 years ago. Her picture hangs on a wall in the bar and whenever the portrait is moved strange events are reported. These include disembodied voices, loud footsteps and items being moved or thrown violently around the pub.

STORIES BEHIND THE WALK

☆ **South Tyne Trail** The walk briefly coincides with both the Pennine Way and the South Tyne Trail. The latter is a 23-mile route for walkers and cyclists beside the River South Tyne – from its source near Garrigill to Haltwhistle. The walking trail and the cycle path differ at times, but they mostly follow a shared route along bridleways and quiet country roads. North of the South Tynedale Railway at Slaggyford, they run along the trackbed of a disused section of the line.

☆ **Fairhill Recreation Ground** Once a place where drovers would rest their livestock on the way to market, Fairhill was gifted to the people of Alston as a place of rest and recreation in 1899. Over the years it has hosted circuses, horse shows, gala days and markets, and continues to be a venue for May Day celebrations, Halloween parties and other family events.

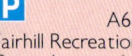

Fairhill Recreation Ground

½ mile

🅿 Fairhill Recreation Ground car park

A689 🚗 Swans Head antiques

- Leave the car park via the pedestrian access (left of vehicle entrance).
- Turn **left** along the pavement.
- At the T-junction at the bottom, turn **right**, watching carefully for Swans Head antiques in a few yards on the left. Cross the main road.

❶
- Turn sharp **left** – almost back on yourself – on an asphalt path between buildings.
- Keep **left** in 50 yards at a fork.
- On reaching a lane, go **left** and then take the next **right**, walking ⅓ mile to a fingerpost and wall stile (right).

36 Short Walks Made Easy

🚂 South Tynedale Railway In the mid-19th century, a 14-mile branch line was built connecting Alston with the main Carlisle to Newcastle railway line at Haltwhistle. This was constructed mainly to serve the area's lead and coal mines, although it continued to serve as a passenger railway until its closure in 1976. The southern end of it has since been converted to a narrow-gauge heritage line, the South Tynedale Railway. Scheduled services run along a five-mile stretch of line from Alston to Slaggyford (south-tynedale-railway.org.uk).

☆ **Alston on screen**
It's hardly surprising that, when looking for somewhere that's changed little in appearance over the last 200 years or so, programme makers are often won over by the town's cobbled lanes, traditional shop fronts and beautiful stone buildings. In 1996, scenes for an ITV adaptation of *Jane Eyre* were filmed here and, three years later, the cameras were rolling again when Alston was transformed into the coastal town of Bruntmarsh for a TV mini-series of Dickens' classic novel *Oliver Twist*.

2 ➤ Turn **right** over the stile – signposted Firs Walk.
➤ Descend the field edge on a faint, grassy trail beside a walled woodland (right) for 200 yards to another wall stile.

3 ➤ **Cross** the stile to enter the woods.
➤ After a small bridge, walk downhill. *Beware exposed tree roots.*
➤ Meeting the Pennine Way, turn **right** along it for nearly ½ mile to a path junction after a hostel (right).

NATURE NOTES

As the walk heads out of Alston along Strait Loaning, the path is fringed by beech hedges and elder. Further out of town, as the views over the surrounding countryside open out, rowan can be seen growing beside the walled track.

Beyond the stile at ❸, the field edge contains ragwort, clover, butterbur, great burnet and other species common to uncultivated ground, while the woodland is rich with rowan, ash, Scots pine, beech and sycamore. Watch for well-camouflaged treecreepers spiralling up the tree trunks, using their long, downcurved bills to search the bark for insects.

Where the route coincides with the Pennine Way and the South Tyne Trail, the steep embankment on the left is cloaked with beech, oak and sycamore, while the path itself is fringed by blackthorn and hawthorn. Watch for a spooky, bearded face that has been elaborately carved into an old tree trunk.

Pennine Way and South Tyne Trail — **South Tyne Trail**
Hostel (right) — ❹ — A686 — 1½ miles

❹ ▸ Leave the Pennine Way when it drops left through trees; instead, bear **left** along a surfaced track, soon reaching a road.
▸ Go **left** and follow it down to a main road.
▸ **Cross** over, turn **right** then keep **ahead** along a pavement to the South Tynedale Railway turning in ¼ mile.

❺ ▸ Go **left** along the South Tynedale Railway's access lane.
▸ After visiting, return to the main road and turn **right**, retracing steps for almost 150 yards to an alley (Burn Bank) on the left.

Above: sloes

Top: elderberries Bottom: ragwort

6 ➤ Turn **left** up the alley, rising between walls.
➤ Climb steps at the top and continue **straight ahead** along a lane.
➤ Follow this round to the **right** and then turn **right** along another walled alley, passing a church (right).

7 ➤ Emerging onto cobbles, keep **straight on** and then swing **right** to climb to the Market Cross.
➤ Turn **left** along the main road, rising for 100 yards to a turning on the left just after the road narrows.

8 ➤ Turn **left** and follow the road round to meet the main road (A689).
➤ Go **left** at the junction, and the car park entrance lies up the hill on the right.

Walk 4 Alston 39

Opposite (clockwise): peacock butterfly; roe deer; oyster mushroom; hawthorn flowers
This page (clockwise): rowan berries; wigeon; autumn colours, Allen Banks

WALK 5

LONG MEG AND HER DAUGHTERS

The highlight of this walk in the beautiful Eden Valley at the western base of the North Pennines is Long Meg and Her Daughters. But there's more to the walk than visiting one of Britain's oldest and largest stone circles. It also calls in on a church that's been separated from its village but has regained several of its ancient artefacts; and it wanders along woodland tracks that are noisy with birdlife, no matter what time of year you visit.

OS information
NY 570367 Explorer OL5
Distance 2.4 miles / 3.8km
Time 1¼ hours
Start/Finish Near Little Salkeld
Parking CA10 1NW Long Meg and Her Daughters car park, ½ mile north-east of Little Salkeld
Public toilets None
Cafés/pubs Nearest in Langwathby, almost 2½ miles south of 🚶: The Shepherds Inn; Saddleback's coffee van (on village green)
Terrain Surfaced lane; field paths, which could be muddy; woodland tracks
Hilliness Gently undulating
Footwear Year round 🥾
Public transport Nearest regular service is the Settle to Carlisle Railway, with Langwathby station 2½ miles south of 🚶: settle-carlisle.co.uk

42 Short Walks Made Easy

Did you know? The flour mill in Little Salkeld is one of Britain's last remaining, independently run, working watermills. It was built as a corn mill in 1745 but became obsolete soon after Carr's built its industrial-scale mill at the port in Silloth, on the Solway coast, in 1836. Having been restored by a local couple in the 1970s, it now produces organic, stoneground flour to order (watermill-holidays.co.uk).

Local legend There are a lot of spooky legends associated with Long Meg and Her Daughters. The stones are said to be the remains of a coven of witches turned to stone by Scottish wizard Michael Scot for using profanities on the Sabbath. It's also claimed that, when local squire Colonel Lacy attempted to destroy the stones in the 18th century, a terrifying storm broke out and the labourers fled in fear of black magic – and never came back.

Walk 5 Long Meg and Her Daughters

STORIES BEHIND THE WALK

+ Addingham church You can search high and low on the Ordnance Survey map of this area for the village of Addingham, but you won't find it. That's because it was washed away when the nearby River Eden changed course in about 1350. The village church, St Michael and All Angels, was reconstructed on its present site in the early 16th century using some of the stone recovered from the original ninth-century building.

☆ **Hammerhead cross**
Just outside the church porch are the remains of a carved, hammerhead cross perforated with four holes. This was also recovered from the original church and probably dates from about the 10th century.

☆ **Norse tombstone**
There are several ancient artefacts within the church porch. These include a Norse hogback tombstone, two pieces of a cross shaft also dating from Norse times, and some coffin lids decorated with early Christian motifs. These were all retrieved from the bed of the River Eden when a drought exposed them in 1913.

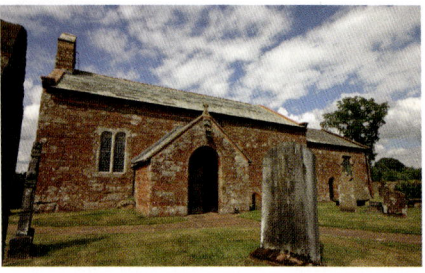

- Leave the car park via the pedestrian exit and turn **right** along a track.
- Immediately, keep **straight ahead** along the lane to the edge of the stone circle in ¼ mile.

1 ▸ At the first of the stones, leave the lane by keeping close to the hedgerow on the **right** to a gate in the field corner in about 150 yards.

⭐ Long Meg and Her Daughters

Dating from the late Neolithic or early Bronze Age, Long Meg and Her Daughters is one of Britain's largest stone circles. Nearly 60 stones remain, the largest being Long Meg herself, a 12-foot monolith that stands just outside the main ring. Constructed of red sandstone quarried from the banks of the River Eden, she bears faint traces of mysterious cup and ring markings as well as concentric circles. These are thought to be 4,500 years old and their meaning is unknown. Seen from the centre of the circle, she is aligned with the midwinter sunset (friendsoflongmeg.com).

❸ Pedestrian gate　　❹ Lane　　1 mile　　❺ Churchyard gate　　Addingham church　　❻ Churchyard gate

☆ Norse tombstone; Hammerhead cross

2 ▶ Go through the pedestrian gate between two metal field gates.
▶ Continue with a hedgerow (right) across a large field to two metal gates on the far side.
▶ Pass through the **right-hand** one and walk along the field's left-hand edge to a pedestrian gate.

3 ▶ Go through the gate to join an enclosed path between a wall and a fence.
▶ After a metal gate, join a short section of farm track.
▶ Go through a pedestrian gate to the **right** of metal farm gates and carry on to a lane.

NATURE NOTES

The hedgerow and light woodland encountered between ❶ and ❹ contain oak, beech, blackthorn, elder, sycamore, hawthorn and bramble. A couple of species that are slightly unusual in this farmland context are the Norway maple and cotoneaster franchetti. Both are non-native, ornamental species more commonly associated with parks and gardens. Scientists at the Royal Horticultural Society recently discovered that the latter is at least 20 per cent more effective at absorbing roadside air pollution than other shrubs.

Birds likely to be encountered include buzzard, rook, wren, robin, chaffinch, jackdaw, great tit, long-tailed tit and the goldcrest, one of Britain's two smallest birds. Listen for its repetitive, high-pitched calls, particularly in areas with conifer trees.

Soon after ❷, there is a small ash tree with a massive burr (or burl) at the base of its trunk. The tree is just to the left of the path. Burrs are usually caused by damage to the trunk or by a virus or fungus.

Opposite page
Top: buzzard
Left: ash tree burr
Middle: bramble
Right: goldcrest

Waymarked path junction

❼

1½ miles

❹ ▪ **Cross** the lane and go through the field gate opposite.
▪ Aim straight for the church **ahead** to reach the churchyard gate.

❺ ▪ Enter the churchyard and follow a paved path round the side of the church and out through another gate.

❻ ▪ Immediately turn sharp **left**, almost back on yourself, to walk with the church wall on your left. The stony track quickly becomes a grassy path.
▪ Ignoring side tracks, keep **ahead** for ⅓ mile and descend to a waymarked junction.

46 Short Walks Made Easy

Gate | Longmeg farm buildings (right) | 2 miles | ☆ Long Meg and Her Daughters | Long Meg and Her Daughters car park 🅿

7 ▶ Keep **straight ahead** on the narrower trail that soon bends **left**.
▶ Stay with the leafy way for ⅓ mile to the next gate.

8 ▶ After the gate, continue **straight ahead** on a path beside a fence (left).
▶ Nearing farm buildings, join a lane running to the **left** of sheds.
▶ Pass through the middle of the stone circle and rejoin the outward route to return to 🚶.

Walk 5 Long Meg and Her Daughters

WALK 6

RIVER WEAR AT STANHOPE

The market town of Stanhope lies on the north bank of the River Wear in County Durham. This easy, relaxing walk passes some of the town's historic features, including a fossilised tree stump, the medieval church of St Thomas's and the Weardale Heritage Railway, before reaching the river. As you walk both sides of the rushing waters, you have a chance to listen and watch for the wildlife that calls these wooded banks home.

OS information
NY 995392 Explorer OL31
Distance 2.2 miles/3.5km
Time 1¼ hours
Start/Finish Stanhope
Parking DL13 2FJ Durham Dales Centre car park, Castle Gardens
Public toilets Durham Dales Centre
Cafés/pubs Durham Dales Centre; Stanhope
Terrain Pavement; quiet lanes; field, woodland and riverside paths
Hilliness Gently undulating
Footwear Spring/Autumn/Winter 🥾 Summer 👟

Public transport
Bus service 101, between Bishop Auckland and Stanhope: weardale-travel.co.uk

Accessibility
Suitable for wheelchairs and pushchairs from 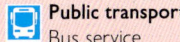 to ② and ⑦ to end

Dogs
Welcome but keep on leads. One step stile without dog gate

Did you know? Stanhope was the site of the last battle in the First War of Scottish Independence. In August 1327, after a three-day standoff, the Scots and the English took positions on opposite sides of the River Wear. James, Lord of Douglas, led a stealthy night-time assault on the English camp, killing several soldiers and cutting the ropes of the English tents. One even collapsed on the leader of the English forces – King Edward III.

Local legend A young girl from near Stanhope came across a group of fairies after she strayed too far from home. She ran back to her parents, but the fairies came in the night and kidnapped the girl because she'd seen them. The girl's father was advised to collect impossible-sounding gifts and offerings, including a chicken with no bones. Due to his resourcefulness, he found each gift and was able to exchange them for his daughter.

Walk 6 River Wear at Stanhope

STORIES BEHIND THE WALK

✝ St Thomas's Church Set back from the road, St Thomas's Church was built in Norman times on the site of an earlier church. During the heyday of the lead-mining industry, rectors received a share of the profits, making this a particularly lucrative benefice. Most rectors were Bishops of Durham. Inside, visitors can see a variety of artefacts including a Roman altar and Victorian stained-glass windows.

☆ **Fossil tree** Stanhope's fossilised tree stump is a remnant of the tropical swamp that existed here about 320 million years ago – when the area we now call the North Pennines was almost on the Equator. It was unearthed in a sandstone quarry a few miles north of Stanhope in 1915 and was brought to the village, in large pieces, in the 1960s. Located within the churchyard of St Thomas's, it is best viewed from the road.

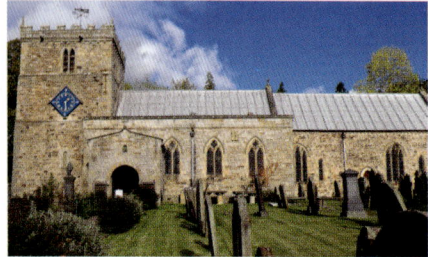

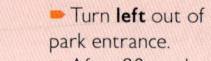
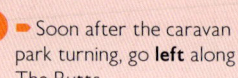
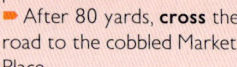

Durham Dales Centre car park

- Turn **left** out of the car park entrance.
- After 80 yards, **cross** the road to the cobbled Market Place.
- Keep **forward** along The Butts, a lane parallel with the main road at a lower level. This swings **right** leading to a caravan park entrance.

①
- Soon after the caravan park turning, go **left** along The Butts.
- Pass through a gate and turn **left** beside the disused railway.
- When the path ends, head **left** and immediately swing **right** along the road towards the station (150 yards).

Short Walks Made Easy

Weardale Heritage Railway

The Weardale Railway started life in 1847 as a 25-mile branch line of the Stockton and Darlington Railway, taking material to Teesside's ironworks. It ran from Bishop Auckland to Wearhead. Passenger services ceased in 1953, but the line continued to serve the Eastgate cement works until 1993. Since then, volunteers have restored a 16-mile section from Bishop Auckland to Stanhope, running heritage services and preserving rolling stock (weardale-railway.org.uk).

☆ River Wear

The River Wear rises in the North Pennines, close to the Killhope Lead Mining Museum. It then flows through Stanhope, Wolsingham, Bishop Auckland and Durham before entering the North Sea at Sunderland – a total distance of about 60 miles. For much of its journey, it is followed by the Weardale Way, a 45-mile walking route from Cowshill to Sunderland Bridge. Other major rivers of the north-east also rise in the North Pennines, including the River Tees and the River South Tyne.

Kissing-gate ❸

Wall stile/Lane ❹

Road bridge over railway

1 mile

Road bridge over River Wear

Heather View Leisure Park

☆ River Wear

❷ ▸ Just before the station buildings, take the signposted path **right**.
▸ **Cross** a footbridge over the railway.
▸ Pass through a kissing-gate then turn **left** to walk beside a fence (left) along the edge of a large field to a kissing-gate in its far corner.

❸ ▸ Go through the kissing-gate, cross the railway and turn **right**, joining a riverside path.
▸ Keep **left** at a faint fork, soon entering a field.
▸ Walk with a fence (right) to reach a wall stile.

Walk 6 River Wear at Stanhope

NATURE NOTES

It is from the paths beside the River Wear that you are most likely to encounter wildlife on this walk, particularly along the more wooded sections. Here, small birds such as chaffinches, blue tits, robins and nuthatches move from tree to tree; listen out too for the 'tik-tik' of wrens. More likely to be heard than seen, wrens favour hollows such as gaps in drystone walls or crevices in trees created by fallen branches. The river itself is the haunt of dipper, mallard and heron.

Tree species include sycamore, ash, oak, hazel and some conifers. There's a particularly fine row of massive, mature trees beside the surfaced riverside path leading to **8**. These include horse chestnut and beech. Watch too for ivy growing up tree trunks, dog rose and hawthorn.

Look out for toads on quiet lanes and paths. The key to telling the difference between a frog and a common toad is the skin texture – toads have a dry, warty appearance while frogs are smooth and slimy.

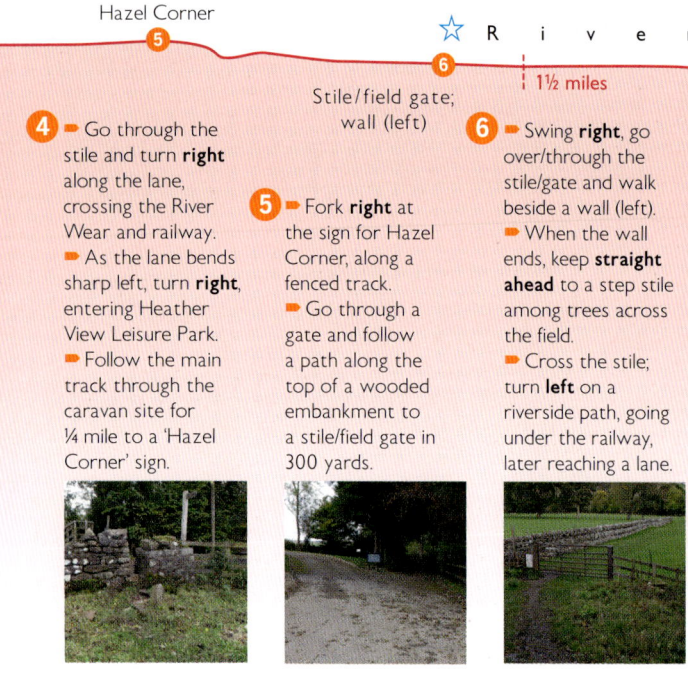

Hazel Corner **5**

Stile/field gate; wall (left)

River **6**

1½ miles

4 ▪ Go through the stile and turn **right** along the lane, crossing the River Wear and railway.
▪ As the lane bends sharp left, turn **right**, entering Heather View Leisure Park.
▪ Follow the main track through the caravan site for ¼ mile to a 'Hazel Corner' sign.

5 ▪ Fork **right** at the sign for Hazel Corner, along a fenced track.
▪ Go through a gate and follow a path along the top of a wooded embankment to a stile/field gate in 300 yards.

6 ▪ Swing **right**, go over/through the stile/gate and walk beside a wall (left).
▪ When the wall ends, keep **straight ahead** to a step stile among trees across the field.
▪ Cross the stile; turn **left** on a riverside path, going under the railway, later reaching a lane.

52 Short Walks Made Easy

Above: acorns
Below: wren

Above: toad
Below: dog rose

St Thomas's Church

Fossil tree

2 miles

Durham Dales Centre car park

7 ➡ Keep **straight ahead** on the lane to a footbridge over the River Wear.
➡ Turn **right** to cross the bridge.
➡ Turn **right** along a riverside path on the opposite bank, walking to bollards at the path's end.

8 ➡ After the bollards, bear **left**.
➡ Keep **straight ahead** along the lane, rejoining the outward route at **1**.
➡ Retrace your steps back to the car park.

Walk 6 River Wear at Stanhope 53

WALK 7

DUFTON

The pretty, red sandstone village of Dufton lies in the Eden Valley, close to the point where the land begins rising towards the Pennines' western escarpment. Close to High Cup, on the route of the Pennine Way, and with some beautiful low-lying countryside too, it's long been a popular spot for walkers. This walk explores the wooded gorge of Dufton Ghyll before heading out along lanes and tracks that lead closer to the foot of the Pennine heights.

OS information

NY 689 249
Explorer OL19

Distance
2.1 miles/3.4km

Time
1¼ hours

Start/Finish
Dufton

Parking CA16 6DB
Dufton village car park (honesty box)

Public toilets
In the car park

Cafés/pubs
Post Box Pantry café; The Stag Inn, both in Dufton

Terrain
Woodland paths, potentially muddy; stony farm and village tracks; cobbles; village road (no pavement)

Hilliness
Undulating, but with steady rather than steep ups and downs

Footwear Year round	
Public transport None	
Accessibility Only village road suitable for wheelchairs; all-terrain pushchairs from to ②	
Dogs Welcome but keep on leads. No stiles	

Did you know? Many walkers use Dufton as the start point for visiting High Cup. This impressive, U-shaped valley is one of the most famous geological features in the entire Pennine chain. The sides of the massive trench are rimmed by huge columns of dolerite rock, known as the Whin Sill. This line of rock runs through the North Pennines and Northumberland. Much of Hadrian's Wall was built along the crest of its undulating ridge.

Local legend Cross Fell, which dominates the skyline in this part of the Eden Valley, was once known as Fiend's Fell. This is possibly due to the howling noise that results when Britain's only named wind – the Helm Wind – blows. It is reputed to have the force to send people and livestock flying through the air. According to legend, the name Cross Fell derives from a blessing given by Saint Augustine to banish the 'fiend'.

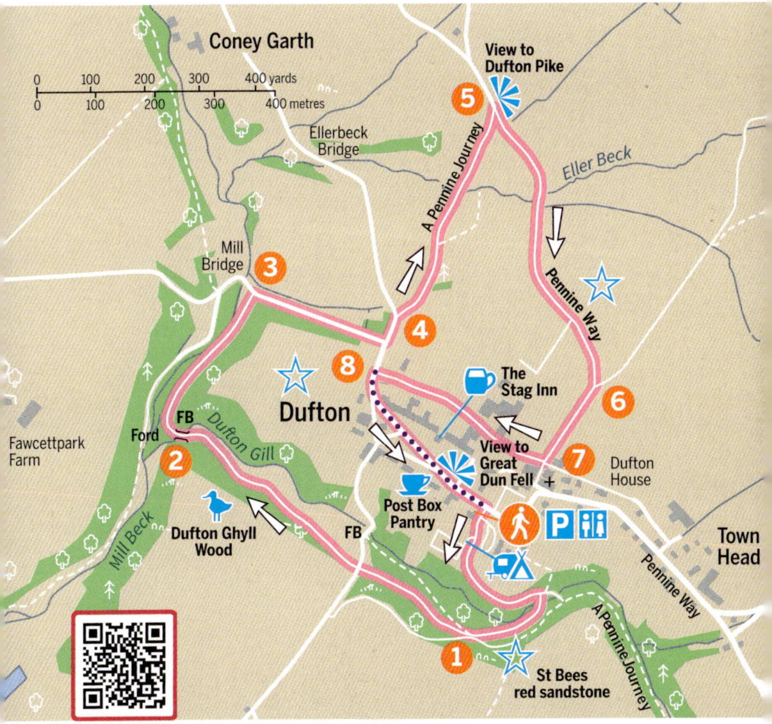

Walk 7 Dufton

STORIES BEHIND THE WALK

Dufton Pike Dufton Pike is one of several distinctive, conical hills at the foot of the main Pennine escarpment. These are composed of volcanic rocks and slates that formed between 480 and 420 million years ago. They are the oldest rocks found in the North Pennines. The most common rocks in the region, found above these ones, date from the Carboniferous period, about 360 to 300 million years ago. These are mostly limestone, shale and sandstone.

Pennine Way From ⑤ to ⑦, the walk follows the route of the Pennine Way, a 268-mile national trail from Edale in Derbyshire to Kirk Yetholm in the Scottish Borders. The idea for the long-distance walk was first mooted by Tom Stephenson in 1935 and he started devising a route using existing paths. However, 70 miles of new rights of way were also required, so it wasn't until 1965 that Britain's first national trail could be officially opened.

Dufton — Dufton Gill — St Bees red sandstone — ½ mile

Dufton village car park — **D u f t o n   G h y l l   W o o d**

- Turn **right** out of the car park and immediately **right** again along a campsite track.
- After dropping to cross the beck in wooded Dufton Ghyll, follow the track round a right-hand bend to a fork in 175 yards.

① - Where the path splits, branch **right**, signed to Mill Bridge.
- Go **straight over** a crossing of paths in a shallow dip and keep **ahead** for just under ¼ mile to a wooden footbridge.

56 Short Walks Made Easy

☆ Dufton

Lead was mined from the fellsides above Dufton for many centuries, with the mines being taken over by the London Lead Company in the 1820s. Like many other Quaker-run firms, the London Lead Company provided facilities for its workers and their families. In Dufton, this included building homes, helping to reopen the village school and providing a clean water supply. The fountain on the village green, for example, was installed in 1858 (picture page 27).

☀ Great Dun Fell

High up in the Pennines, on top of Great Dun Fell, is a golfball-like structure, a radome, that is visible from several points on this walk. This is part of the Civil Aviation Authority's air traffic control system. It provides radar and radio cover for air traffic over northern England and the North Sea, covering a radius of about 250 miles. Construction began in 1985 and it was commissioned in early 1987, later than anticipated because of the harsh weather workers experienced on the summit.

Dufton Gill footbridge ❷   Mill Beck   Wooden gate ❸   1 mile ❹

❷ ▶ Cross the footbridge and keep **straight ahead**, following the clearest path to a gate in about 350 yards.

❸ ▶ Go through the wooden gate and turn **right** along a lane.
▶ Turn **left** at a T-junction at the top of the climb and watch for a turning on the right in 50 yards.

NATURE NOTES

Dufton Ghyll slices through an area of St Bees red sandstone, with the rock exposed in several places. The slopes are cloaked in thick, semi-natural woodland that includes beech, oak, sweet chestnut, sycamore and some elm. The Woodand Trust has managed the site since 1980 and has added to the existing mature trees by planting more native broadleaf species. Some of the younger trees include birch, rowan, hazel and cherry. The woodland floor is rich with wood anemone, winter aconite, pignut, snowdrop and bluebell. Mosses, ferns and liverworts thrive in the old quarries. Roe deer frequent the woods and red squirrels are still spotted from time to time, although their numbers are dwindling. Watch for heron beside the beck.

Hawthorn flanks the route of the Pennine Way from ❺ onwards, its white, springtime flowers known as May blossom.

The road through the middle of the village green is lined by lime trees, planted here in 1892. Benches under the trees provide welcome shade on a hot summer's day.

Lime trees in Dufton

View to Dufton Pike

Pennine Way
1½ miles

❹ ■ Turn **right** along the track.
■ After ¼ mile, the track bends left. Leave it here by turning sharp **right** along the signposted Pennine Way.

❺ ■ Follow the Pennine Way, crossing clapper-style bridges to a path T-junction in ⅓ mile.

❻ ■ Turn **right** at the T-junction with the enclosed track.
■ In 175 yards, immediately before the first building on the right, turn **right** along a cobbled track.

Above: hawthorn flowers
Below: bluebells

Top: St Bees red sandstone
Bottom: heron

The Stag Inn (left)
View to Great Dun Fell
Dufton
2 miles
Post Box Pantry (right)
Dufton village car park

7 ▸ Keep **straight on**, through gates, to cross a farmyard.
▸ Carry on for 250 yards to a road.

8 ▸ Turn **left** along the road. This bends left and passes through the middle of Dufton.
▸ The car park entrance is on the **right** soon after the village green.

Walk 7 Dufton

DRURY
TEA & COFFEE

VIS VNITA FORTIOR
THE LORD CREWE ARMS

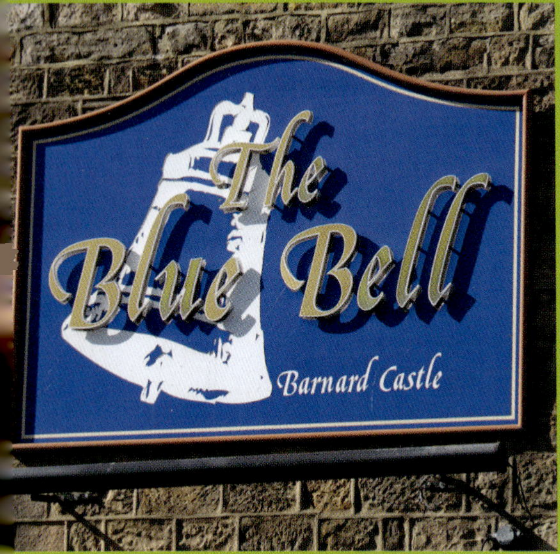
The Blue Bell
Barnard Castle

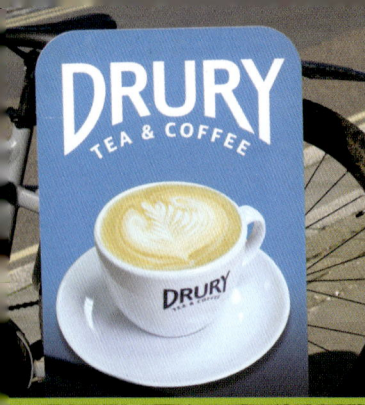

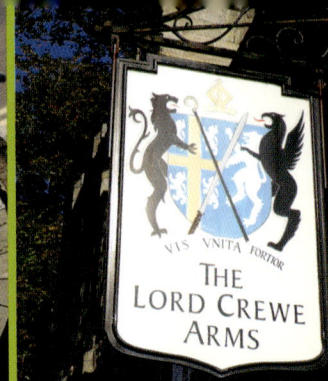

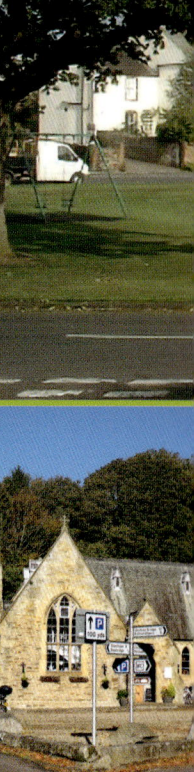

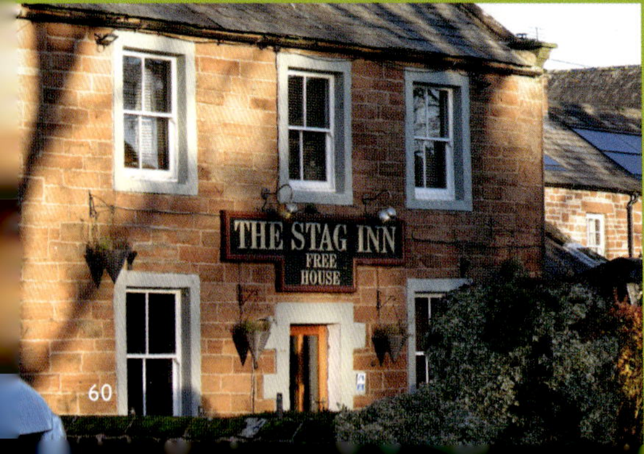
THE STAG INN
FREE HOUSE

This page (clockwise): Café at South Tynedale railway station, Alston; The Shepherds Inn, Langwathby; Bowlees Visitor Centre; The White Monk Refectory, Blanchland
Opposite page (clockwise): Barnard Castle; The Lord Crewe Arms, Blanchland; The Stag Inn, Dufton; The Blue Bell, Barnard Castle

WALK 8

HIGH FORCE AND LOW FORCE

High Force is one of Britain's most spectacular waterfalls. As the River Tees comes roaring down from the high fells, it plunges 70 feet over an almost vertical rock face, creating a powerful, whitewater spectacle. Many visitors take the private path on the north side of the river but, in so doing, miss out on another impressive falls at Low Force. Crossing a historic suspension bridge and following a riverside section of the Pennine Way, this walk takes in both waterfalls for an unforgettable experience.

OS information
NY 907282
Explorer OL31

Distance
3.9 miles/6.3km

Time
2¼ hours

Start/Finish
Bowlees

Parking DL12 0XE
Bowlees Visitor Centre car park (donations)

Public toilets
In the car park

Cafés/pubs
Café in visitor centre; picnic tables

Terrain
Mostly constructed paths, but with occasional exposed tree roots

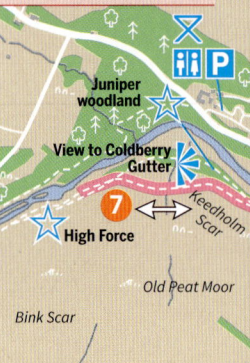

Scan Me

62 *Short Walks Made Easy*

Did you know? Footage of High Force appears in the 1969 Western film *Mackenna's Gold* starring Omar Sharif, Gregory Peck and Telly Savalas. In the film, a raft is destroyed as it is carried over a waterfall by the force of the river's current. The Hollywood stars didn't actually visit the North Pennines to film the river scenes, though; stock footage of the waterfall was used instead.

Local legend The upper reaches of the River Tees are said to be haunted by a water sprite called Peg Powler. She supposedly lived in the valley which now houses Cow Green Reservoir, a few miles upstream of High Force. If the Tees is fierce and frothy, this may be 'Peg Powler's suds', a phenomenon that gives away her presence in the river where she waits to lure the unsuspecting to their watery death.

Hilliness
Mostly gradual ascents/descents but with a steeper section ⑤ to ⑥

Footwear
Spring/Autumn/Winter
Summer

Public transport
None

Accessibility

Unsuitable for wheelchairs or pushchairs

Dogs
Welcome but keep on leads. No stiles

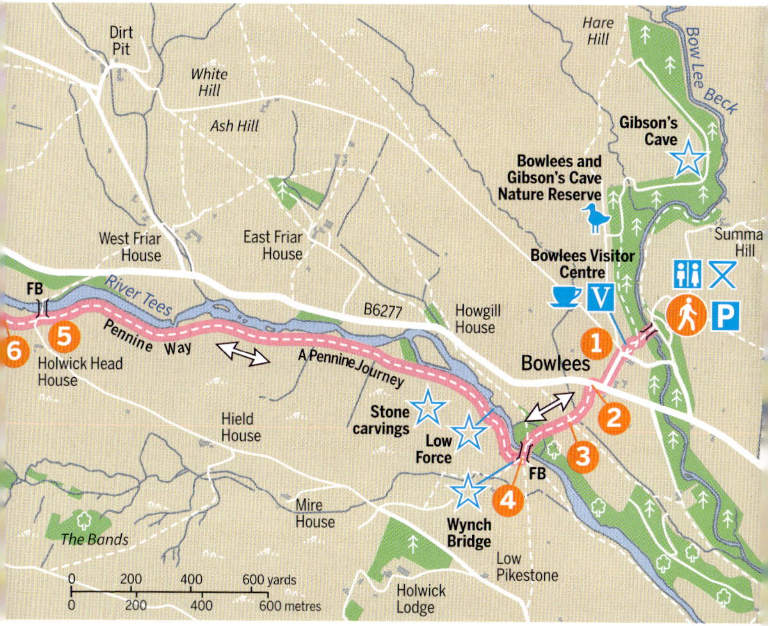

Walk 8 High Force and Low Force

STORIES BEHIND THE WALK

☆ **Wynch Bridge** Built by public subscription in 1741 to enable lead miners to cross the River Tees, Wynch Bridge is one of the earliest suspension bridges of its type in Europe. In 1802, one of the chains snapped as a party of nine haymakers were crossing and the bridge collapsed. Two people fell onto the rocks 60 feet below; one was drowned. The bridge was repaired and then replaced in 1830 by the one that exists today.

Coldberry Gutter As you make your way back down the River Tees after visiting High Force, you will see a distinctive notch on the skyline ahead. This is Coldberry Gutter. It was originally thought to be a hush – created when water is used in mineral exploitation. Recent research suggests, however, that it started life as a geological fault deepened by glacial meltwater that has been only slightly modified by mining operations.

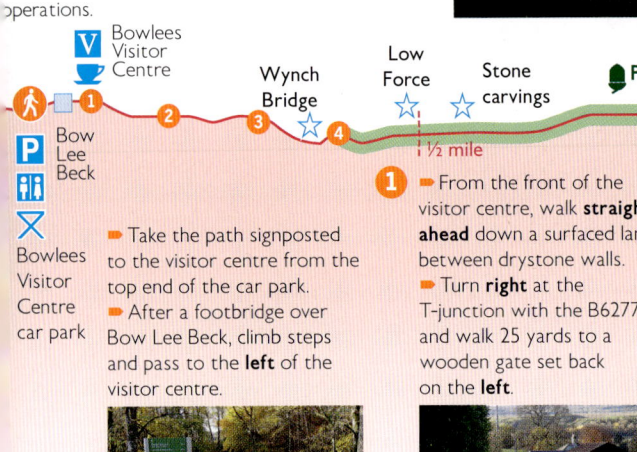

➡ Take the path signposted to the visitor centre from the top end of the car park.
➡ After a footbridge over Bow Lee Beck, climb steps and pass to the **left** of the visitor centre.

① ➡ From the front of the visitor centre, walk **straight ahead** down a surfaced lane between drystone walls.
➡ Turn **right** at the T-junction with the B6277 and walk 25 yards to a wooden gate set back on the **left**.

64 Short Walks Made Easy

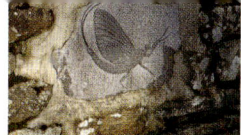

☆ Stone carvings

As you make your way along the riverside path, you will see a number of stone carvings in the walls. They show two of the aquatic insects found in the River Tees – the mayfly and stonefly – in their nymph and adult forms. They were carved out of black Weardale limestone by Newcastle-born sculptor Peter Graham as part of the 'Cold Blooded and Spineless' project organised by the North Pennines AONB (now the North Pennines National Landscape).

☆ The waterfalls

The waterfalls of High Force and Low Force occur where the River Tees drops over the Whin Sill, a line of volcanic rock that was formed underground about 295 million years ago. Since the end of the last glacial period, water has been eroding the softer layers of limestone and sandstone lower down in the cliff leaving the more hard-wearing lip of volcanic rock. As the more resistant rock is undercut, blocks of it fall away, causing the waterfall to retreat upstream.

1½ miles ☆
6
Footbridge (keep left)   First kissing-gate   Juniper woodland   Second kissing-gate
5

1 mile

R i v e r   T e e s

2 ▶ Pass through the gate and follow a surfaced path through two meadows to reach a wooden gate, to the right of a squeeze stile in a wall.

3 ▶ Go through the gate and enter a wooded area.
▶ Keep **forward**, ignoring a path (right), and descend steps to reach the River Tees.
▶ **Cross** Wynch Bridge

Walk 8 High Force and Low Force

NATURE NOTES

The mature woodland around Low Force and Wynch Bridge is dominated by beech trees and Scots pine. If the noise of Low Force isn't drowning them out, listen for a variety of birds including long-tailed tits, chaffinches, blue tits, wrens and treecreepers. Watch for mallards and dippers on the river. The riverside path is fringed by birch and rowan, and wildflowers here include globeflower, melancholy thistle, bird's-foot trefoil and shrubby cinquefoil.

Beyond the kissing-gate at ❻, the walk enters the largest area of juniper woodland left in England. Juniper is one of only three conifers that are native to Britain, the other two being Scots pine and yew. Juniper berries are used to flavour gin and, in the 17th century, the herbalist Nicholas Culpepper recommended them as a treatment for asthma and sciatica and for speeding up childbirth. Sadly, this area of juniper is infected with *phytophthora austrocedri*, a pathogen that prevents the tree from taking up water through its roots, eventually killing it.

Juniper

High Force ❼ — 2 miles
Juniper woodland
View to Coldberry Gutter (ahead)
Footbridge (keep right) — 2½ miles
Pennine Way

River Tees

❹ ▸ Bear **right**, up some stone steps.
▸ Follow the path upstream beside the river, soon drawing level with Low Force.
▸ *Take care: the riverside path is uneven, with exposed tree roots and bedrock.* Keep going to the next footbridge in 1 mile.

❺ ▸ At the footbridge, keep **left** to stay on the south bank.
▸ A stony path climbs slightly and soon leads to the first of two kissing-gates.

66 Short Walks Made Easy

Top left: long-tailed tit
Bottom left: dipper
Above: globeflower
Below: melancholy thistle

6 ➤ Go through the gate.
➤ About 300 yards after the second kissing-gate, keep your eyes peeled for an easy-to-miss fork in the path.

7 ➤ Bear **right** at the fork to reach the High Force viewing platform in 50 yards.
➤ After enjoying the spectacle, return by reversing your outward route, remembering to turn **right** at the B6277 and immediately **left** to reach the visitor centre.

Walk 8 High Force and Low Force   67

WALK 9

HURY RESERVOIR

Whether it's a river, the sea, a lake or a reservoir, it's always a joy to walk in the company of water – and this route is no exception. It completes a circuit of Hury Reservoir, one of a chain of reservoirs in Baldersdale, a side valley of Teesdale. It's a remote spot, surrounded by drystone-walled enclosures and meadows where sheep graze and colourful wildflowers thrive. Visit any time of year for an atmospheric but relatively easy stroll.

OS information
NY 965196
Explorer OL31

Distance
3 miles/4.8km

Time
1½ hours

Start/Finish
Near Hury in Baldersdale

Parking DL12 9UU
Car park at the northern end of Hury Reservoir's main dam

Public toilets
In the car park

Cafés/pubs
Picnic tables at ⓘ and ⑧. Nearest pubs in Cotherstone, 3 miles to the east

Terrain
Mostly on grass; a wide path crosses the top of the dam

Hilliness
Almost flat

Footwear
Spring/Autumn/Winter 🥾
Summer 👟

Public transport
None.

Accessibility
....
Unsuitable for wheelchairs or pushchairs

Dogs Welcome but keep on leads. No stiles

Hannah's Meadow Nature Reserve, Low Birk Hatt, Baldersdale

Did you know? Baldersdale was the home of farmer Hannah Hauxwell, who became famous in the 1970s and '80s after appearing on TV documentaries. With no electricity or running water, Hannah ran the family farm single-handedly for many years. It was a hard life made harder by the Pennine winters, but it was one that captured the imaginations of well-wishers from around the world who sent her gifts and money. Hannah died in 2018 at the age of 91.

Local legend A chapel once stood at the southern end of the bridge over the River Tees at nearby Eggleston. Founded by Thomas Newleyne, Rector of Romaldkirk, it was abandoned in the 16th century and demolished in the 17th. Since its demolition there have been reports of a mysterious hooded monk haunting the bridge. Wearing brown robes, he appears to be searching for something on the riverbank.

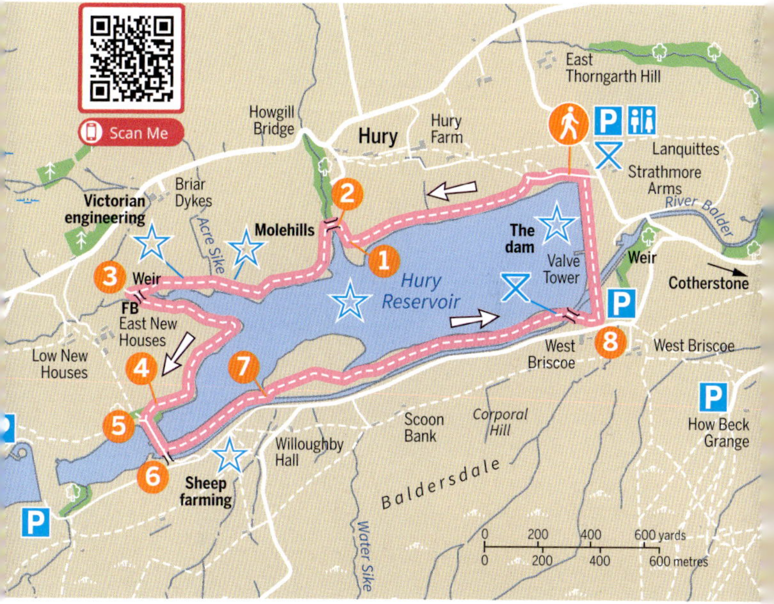

Walk 9 Hury Reservoir 69

STORIES BEHIND THE WALK

☆ **Hury Reservoir** Located in Baldersdale, Hury Reservoir is the lowest of a chain of three, the other two being Blackton and Balderhead, all of which are owned by Northumbrian Water. They are fed by the River Balder, which rises on the soggy moorland of Stainmore Common to the west. As well as being a popular destination for local walkers, Hury Reservoir is stocked weekly with trout, making it ideal for fly-fishing enthusiasts.

☆ **The dam** Several reservoirs were created in Baldersdale and neighbouring Lunesdale, but the Hury dam – 108 feet high and 411 yards long – was the first to be built. It was constructed in the 1890s to supply water to industrial users on Teesside. The engineer was the Lancaster-born James Mansergh who had already worked on a major reservoir project supplying water to Birmingham.

☆ Hury Reservoir

- From the car park, walk up the track – the reservoir fence, left.
- Go through the third gate in this fence.
- Head towards the reservoir and swing **right**, walking with a wall (right) for almost ½ mile to a wall corner.

①
- Go through the gate near the wall corner.
- Follow the wall gently uphill for 75 yards to draw level with a metal gate in a wall.

☆ **Victorian engineering** As you circuit the reservoir, you'll notice that this is not a natural landscape. As well as the dam itself, you'll see the valve tower, which is used to regulate the flow of water downstream. Nearing the western end of the reservoir, watch for stone pillars about 13 feet tall on the hillside. These are air shafts for the aqueduct linking Grassholme Reservoir in Lunesdale with Hury Reservoir. You'll also pass an engineer's survey column, pictured, near the weir between ② and ③.

☆ **Sheep farming** Like much of the North Pennines, Baldersdale is an area with lots of sheep farms. Ewes are mated with rams (sometimes referred to as 'tups') during October and November, so that lambs are born in late winter and early spring. On upland farms such as those in the Pennines, many lambs are born outside, although some may be given shelter for the first few days of their lives.

Molehills ☆ | 1 mile | ③ Second waymarker post
☆ Victorian engineering | Bridge

② ▪ Drop **left** to cross a bridge.
▪ Bear **left**, continuing round the reservoir (water on the left) for ½ mile then pass above a weir, in the direction shown by a waymarker post.
▪ Continue to a second post.

③ ▪ At the second post, drop **left** slightly. In 50 yards switch-back **left** and drop to a footbridge.
▪ **Cross** the bridge and bear **left**.
▪ Continue beside a wall for almost ½ mile, ultimately reaching a fenced woodland corner at the top of a short rise.

NATURE NOTES

Meadow buttercup

The waterfowl that can be seen on Hury Reservoir include teal, wigeon, goosander and tufted duck. In spring, listen for waders such as curlew, snipe and lapwing calling from the surrounding hillsides. In autumn, watch for black grouse in the fields above the south shore. The North Pennines is one of the few areas in England where these endangered birds can still be seen. If you're here late in the day during autumn or winter, you might see flocks of common gulls coming in to roost. More common species include robin, blue tit and rook.

There are lots of wildflowers in the pastures above the reservoir and some of these can be seen along the shore path too. One of the most common is the meadow buttercup. You'll also spot molehills, but you're unlikely to spot the creatures that created these piles of earth because they spend much of their lives underground.

4 ▬ Follow the fence round to the **left** for 20 yards.
▬ When it bends left again, keep **straight ahead** on a faint trail, dropping towards a gate on the far side of a circular structure.

5 ▬ Go through the gate and turn **left** along the top of a dam dividing two sections of the reservoir to the far side.

6 ▬ Just before a bridge, pass through the large gate on the **left**.
▬ Walk to a gate beyond a fenced section of path in ¼ mile, along a narrow strip of land between the reservoir and a concrete channel.

Top: molehills
Middle: lapwing
Bottom: rook

Tufted duck

 Bridge 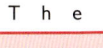 The dam 3 miles
2½ miles

☆ Hury Reservoir

7 ▸ Immediately after the gate, veer **left** to climb beside a fence.
▸ Bear **right** when the path splits at the top.
▸ Reaching picnic benches in ⅔ mile, cross a bridge on the **right** and follow the path into a car park.

8 ▸ On the car park's far side, turn **left** on a path beside a garden fence (right).
▸ Go through the gate to cross the dam.
▸ The gate at the far end of the dam leads back into the car park.

Walk 9 Hury Reservoir 73

WALK 10

RIVER TEES AT BARNARD CASTLE

As well as enjoying some lovely, tree-lined paths beside the River Tees, this walk provides opportunities to explore the attractive County Durham market town of Barnard Castle, known affectionately by local people as Barney. Interesting sights en route include the Butter Market, various historical buildings in the town centre and Bow Bridge. The total walk distance covers two short detours – one to the romantic ruins of Egglestone Abbey (free entry), the other to the Bowes Museum, housed in a French-style chateau.

Did you know? A blue plaque on Market Place marks the site of The King's Head, where novelist Charles Dickens stayed during a visit to Barnard Castle in 1838. In nearby Bowes he found the inspiration for *Nicholas Nickleby*'s Dotheboys Hall and its abusive headmaster

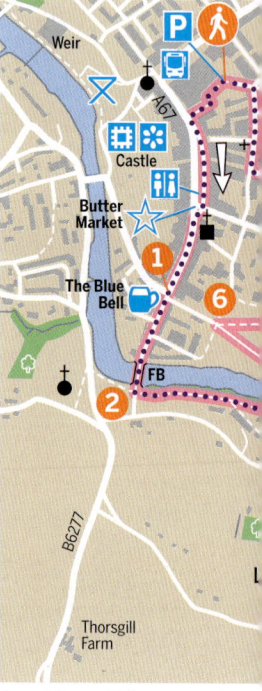

Local legend Blagraves, the oldest house in Barnard Castle and until recently a shop and restaurant, was once visited by Oliver Cromwell. After eating and drinking his fill, he retired to his room for the night where he was plagued by

74   Short Walks Made Easy

Wackford Squeers. The Bowes Academy, run by William Shaw, was notorious for its insanitary conditions and poor educational standards, and some academics believe Dickens based the hard regime of his fictional school on Shaw's institution.

a dozen bone thin ghosts'. Legend also has it that the 15th-century building's cellar is the site of several secret tunnels which run to the castle and Egglestone Abbey. Blagraves is on the route, just after passing the Butter Market.

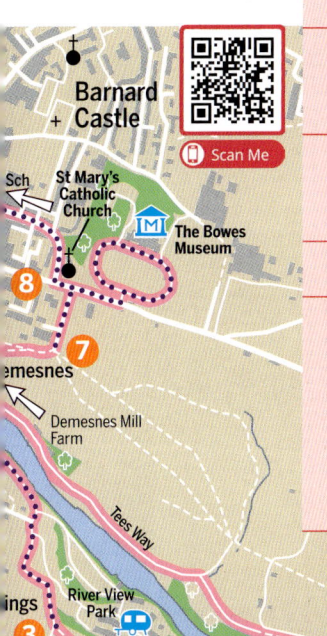

OS information

NZ 051165
Explorer OL31

Distance
4.4 miles/7.1km

Time
2½ hours

Start/Finish
Barnard Castle

Parking DL12 8JJ
Galgate pay & display car park, beside Morrisons

Public toilets
On Market Place (passed soon after 🚶)

Cafés/pubs
Barnard Castle

Terrain
Pavement through town; some surfaced riverside paths, but mostly on grass; quiet lane; exposed tree roots and bedrock immediately after 5

Hilliness
Mildly undulating, with one steep descent on pavement after Butter Market and one steep ascent approaching 3

Footwear
Spring/Autumn/Winter 🥾
Summer 👢

Public transport
Bus services 95, to Middleton-in-Teesdale, and 85, to Bishop Auckland: weardale-travel.co.uk; X75/76, to Darlington, and 6, to Durham: arrivabus.co.uk/north-east; 79, to Richmond: hodgsonsbuses.com

Accessibility
Suitable for robust, powered wheelchairs and all-terrain pushchairs 🚶 to 3, from 4 to 5, and 7 to end

Dogs
Welcome, but keep on leads. No step stiles

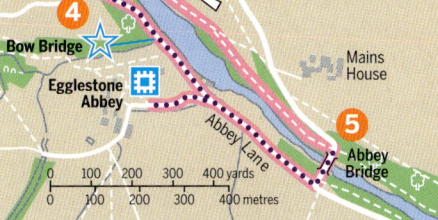

Walk 10 River Tees at Barnard Castle

STORIES BEHIND THE WALK

☆ **Butter Market** The octagonal Butter Market in Barnard Castle is sometimes referred to as the Market Cross or Breaks' Folly. Since being built by wool merchant Thomas Breaks in 1747, it has performed many functions including: a jail, a courtroom, a fire station, a toll booth, a town hall and a dairy market.

☆ **Bow Bridge** The 17th-century Bow Bridge, also known as Thorsgill Beck packhorse bridge, is located on the south side of Abbey Lane soon after ④. The Grade II-listed structure consists of a single arch with low, flat-topped parapets that would have allowed heavily laden ponies to cross easily. The road itself crosses the beck on a more modern bridge just a few feet to the east.

- From the car park's bottom corner, take a pedestrian passageway between single-storey buildings.
- Emerging onto the main shopping street, go **left** along it.
- Keep **straight on** at the octagonal Butter Market to a junction by The Blue Bell in 200 yards.

① - At the junction, keep **straight ahead** – along Thorngate.
- Pass between converted mill buildings at the bottom of the street.
- **Cross** the footbridge over the River Tees.

Short Walks Made Easy

🏛 Egglestone Abbey

The small monastery at Egglestone was established at the end of the 12th century. It was set up by Premonstratensian monks, known as the 'white canons' because of the colour of their habits. After Henry VIII's Dissolution of the Monasteries, the new owner, Robert Strelley, converted part of the site into a mansion. Now in ruins, it is managed by English Heritage and is open to the public throughout the year (english-heritage.org.uk).

🏛 Bowes Museum

This elegant house was built as a public gallery in the 19th century by the illegitimate son of the 10th Earl of Strathmore. It still performs the same function today, housing some internationally important art collections. Painters whose work is on display include Goya, Canaletto and El Greco. The museum is set in extensive grounds with formal gardens and a network of paths through the woodland. Open throughout the year, it also has a café (thebowesmuseum.org.uk).

Abbey Lane **4** — Bow Bridge — 🏛 Egglestone Abbey — Abbey Bridge (River Tees) **5**
1½ miles — 2 miles

2 ➤ Turn **left** along the riverside path; when it splits keep **left**.
➤ In 350 yards, at a T-junction of tracks in a caravan park, turn **right**, uphill.
➤ Climb away, ignoring all left turnings, to a pedestrian gate in another 350 yards.

3 ➤ Turn **left** and pass through the wooden gate.
➤ The path climbs a grassy slope and goes through a hedge gap.
➤ Walk beside fenced woodland (left) across three fields to reach a lane.

NATURE NOTES

On the paths and tracks beside the River Tees you can see trees such as hawthorn, hazel, holly, sycamore, ash, blackthorn, oak, beech, birch and yew, and plants that include common comfrey and butterbur. Walls are covered with ivy, moss and even the long fronds of maidenhair spleenwort. This is a small fern that occurs in a very wide range of habitats all around the world, from Hawaii to the Himalaya and from Africa to Australia.

Birds include many common species such as woodpigeon, blackbird, song thrush and great tit. Watch for heron and mallard on the river. In autumn and winter, flocks of fieldfare and redwing, two migrants in the thrush family, flit from tree to tree, stripping them of berries.

Meadow cranesbill grows along the verges of Abbey Lane. These hardy geraniums flower for several months, offering a long season for pollinators such as bees and solitary wasps.

Above: redwing

4 ▶ Turn **left** along Abbey Lane.
▶ For the 300-yard detour to Egglestone Abbey, turn **right** at the next lane junction (opposite Abbey Mill House); otherwise, keep **straight on**.
▶ At the traffic lights, turn **left** to cross Abbey Bridge.

5 ▶ On the far side, go through a gap in a low wall on the **left** to follow a woodland path.
▶ Leave the woods via a kissing-gate and continue with the river (left) for ¾ mile.
▶ Soon after a gate, join a gravel track between buildings, leading across a recreation field to a fingerpost.

Top left: wood pigeon
Bottom left: fieldfare
Top: maidenhair spleenwort
Middle: holly berries
Bottom: meadow cranesbill

6 ▶ At the fingerpost, turn sharp **right** across grass (no path), passing **right** of a play area.
▶ Climb a short, grassy embankment (path more obvious).
▶ Go **straight over** a crossing path, soon joining another path from the left, walking to the next junction in 100 yards.

7 ▶ Turn **left** through a gate and follow the walled lane to a main road.
▶ For a brief detour to the Bowes Museum, turn **right** and then **left** into the entrance; otherwise, turn **left** along the pavement to the next junction by St Mary's Catholic Church.

8 ▶ Turn **right** onto Birch Road and follow this round a left bend to a T-junction at the end.
▶ Go **right** along Queen Street and pass a school.
▶ Re-enter the car park via an entrance on the **left** in 150 yards.

Walk 10 River Tees at Barnard Castle

Publishing information

© Crown copyright 2024.
All rights reserved.

Ordnance Survey, OS, and the OS logos are registered trademarks, and OS Short Walks Made Easy is a trademark of Ordnance Survey Ltd.

© Crown copyright and database rights (2024) Ordnance Survey.

ISBN 978 0 319092 77 4
1st edition published by Ordnance Survey 2024.

ordnancesurvey.co.uk

While every care has been taken to ensure the accuracy of the route directions, the publishers cannot accept responsibility for errors or omissions, or for changes in details given. The countryside is not static: hedges and fences can be removed, stiles can be replaced by gates, field boundaries can alter, footpaths can be rerouted and changes in ownership can result in the closure or diversion of some concessionary paths. Also, paths that are easy and pleasant for walking in fine conditions may become slippery, muddy and difficult in wet weather.

If you find an inaccuracy in either the text or maps, please contact Ordnance Survey at os.uk/contact.

All rights reserved. No part of this publication may be reproduced, transmitted in any form or by any means, or stored in a retrieval system without either the prior written permission of the publisher, or in the case of reprographic reproduction a licence issued in accordance with the terms and licences issued by the CLA Ltd.

A catalogue record for this book is available from the British Library.

Milestone Publishing credits

Author: Vivienne Crow

Series editor: Kevin Freeborn

Maps: Cosmographics

Design and Production: Patrick Dawson, Milestone Publishing

Printed in India by Replika Press Pvt. Ltd

Photography credits

Front cover: Vivienne Crow.
Back cover: cornfield/Shutterstock.com.

All photographs supplied by the author ©Vivienne Crow except page 6 Mohammed Dhalech (Ordnance Survey); page 22, 25 Kevin Freeborn.

The following images were supplied by Shutterstock.com: page 19 bieszczady_wildlife; 19 Stephen Farhall; 32, 73, 78 Erni; 40 Jordi Jornet; 41 WildMedia; 41 Gertjan Hooijer; 41 Vladimir Ya; 47 Damyan Petkov; 47 Tiuku Laakso; 61 Hazel Platter; 67 Lasse Johansson; 67 SanderMeertinsPhotography; 67 SarahLou Photography; 67 ommi Syvanpera; 69 Paul Gregory; 72 Aghila N; 73 Rudmer Zwerver; 79 Ujhelyi.

The image on pages 60-61 by David Medcalf / Langwathby Village Green / CC BY-SA 2.0, via Wikimedia Commons.